Gumiguru

Togara Muzanenhamo was born in 1975 in Lusaka, Zambia, and grew up on his family's farm in Zimbabwe before studying in the Netherlands and France. His poems have appeared in a number of literary journals. His first collection, *Spirit Brides*, was published by Carcanet in 2006.

Also by Togara Muzanenhamo from Carcanet Press

Spirit Brides

TOGARA MUZANENHAMO

Gumiguru

CARCANET

First published in Great Britain in 2014 by
Carcanet Press Limited
Alliance House
Cross Street
Manchester M2 7AQ

www.carcanet.co.uk

A CIP catalogue record for this book is available from the British Library

ISBN 978 1 84777 257 2

The publisher acknowledges financial assistance from Arts Council England

Typeset by XL Publishing Services, Exmouth
Printed and bound in England by SRP Ltd, Exeter

Aiva madziva ava mazambuko
Aiva mazambuko ava madziva

i.m. S.T.M.

Acknowledgements

Acknowledgements are due to the following journals and organisations, which have published versions of some of these poems: *Almost Island*, Badilisha Poetry Exchange, CNN International, Friends of the Earth, *Granta, KIN, Lamport Court, The Moth, Panorama*, Poetry International, *PN Review*, Radio Netherlands Worldwide, *State of the Nation, Textures, Times Literary Supplement* and World Radio Switzerland.

The author would like to express his gratitude to Lancaster Park, the Ledig-Rowohlt Foundation and the Swiss Arts Council for their support. Some of these poems were worked on while on residency at Château de Lavigny.

Particular thanks to Simon Armitage, Julius Chingono, John Eppel, Mick Imlah, Brian Jones, John Mole, Jane Morris, Murray McCartney, Michael Schmidt, Irene Staunton, Helen Tookey and Musaemura Zimunya.

Contents

Alderflies

Naked and afraid, the girl doubled up with a shrill
that filled the rear-view, the red sun thick off her hair,
her lips peeled back over teeth clenched on tails of air
shredded thin by speed. A rush of rich carmine silt ran
swollen under the bridge, the dry knock of the wheel
pitching the battered Hilux over the ungraded road.
Again her face resurfaced, alone in the mirror, the strain
of the breech birth tightening her breath, the road
rolling stoically to its cruel end where a dirt-strip took
us up to a quiet clinic set at the foot of the mountain.
There, blood and limb turned cold between her thighs.
The drive back home was all silver light and tussock
grass fields, low heavy gears moaning to the turn-off –
the road speckled black, the river's bruised serigraph
woven wet with the brisk evening flight of alderflies.

The Chronicles

for Jessie

They still drew the old roller over the cricket pitches with men
yoked like a team of oxen to the stubborn iron wheel.
The grass smelt as the grass did, all rich beneath the afternoon sun –
the heat flashing off the ground like a blinding flick of steel.
All the fields were there – much smaller than remembered –
the rugby and football grounds unused, the powdered lime lines
washed out by the rains, but the names of dead Jesuits, on signs,
still stood on the preened edges – in traditional white and red.

Up into view the memorable tower of stone rose with all the dreams
of climbing up the winding cool stairwell, up to the top of the turret
where thoughts of fields, soft with warm breaths of red-top, met
the sky with hope and refuge. But those were just a schoolboy's dreams
brought on by the sight of the huge bronze plaque of St George
plunging his spear, extinguishing our fears of the dragon.
Though all that bullshit vanished with age, the hero on the forged
plaque still remained some old myth the Jesuits liked to work on.

'I'm here to go through the Chronicles. '86 to the mid 90s.'
The receptionist is grey and half-deaf, I'm apparently soft-spoken –
so there's a lot of repetition accompanied by grimaces and apologies.
'I'm here to go through the Chronicles.' 'Yes,' to another question,
'I did attend here some years back. Yes, an Old Georgian, an old boy.'
The phone slowly goes up to her ear as she mentions something
about visits and strange requests from foreign journalists wanting
to sit in on classes or have private interviews with the boys.

'Penny? Yes Penny, it's me. I seem to have a safe one here.
Wants to go through the Chronicles. Something about poetry.'
Her small eyes look up. 'You do remember the way to the library?'
I had forgotten, but then retrace the steps in my mind to get there.
Each class I pass, a voice spills from the mock-Edwardian windows,
the red polished floors tap under my feet, and a sweet blessedness
fills me that I'm not sitting in those sweat-rooms of learning, shadows

of my youth, daydreaming about a new world after the first kiss.

The study-hall has lost all its desks and holds an array of instruments and chairs for classical musicians. The fountain in the quad is gone now, and at first it didn't mean a thing to me, but then a crude bewilderment took hold when a memory tried to find its place in the absence; and how on earth they removed it had me lost – the lawn was perfectly smooth. The weights room, where our hands were beaten blue by a leather wad, where iron was pumped on hot afternoons, was now clean and had the smell of sweat and leather replaced by veneered computer booths.

Outside an office, a boy lifted his hat and said 'Good morning' in a way that had me question what he'd said. It was only when I looked back that I noticed the strain on his face, his rheumy eyes and the big black word scoured across his chest, FAGGOT. I could see how easily they could have pinned him down. The tree was there where we sat at break trying to forget the colour bar that still hasn't faded outside the gates; the smell of msasa leaves and old orange peels revived a dead ache that filled my belly: a mob outside the science-labs, fists of other kids...

When I met Penny she smiled, and something told me
it wasn't a strange request to come here and go through the Chronicles.
She had them stacked up on her desk, all piled up chronologically –
towers of memories, names and dates in black and white at my disposal.
I sat down, leafed through the pages, the photographs alive in my head;
and after an hour of being immersed in the vivid quiet, the bell rang:
it was still that same high-pitched drill that once brought relief as it sang
through the long corridors, but also brought with it a certain dread.

All the Good Help

He will not understand her fascination
with rain, these summer months of water
that somehow keep the money coming in,
paying for the nurses his granddaughter

has slowly learnt to trust. Now all the good
help is gone, he feels he can spot liars
with one look; and if he could, he would
take care of her himself. *All these prayers*

for a new body! She doesn't understand
the joke, but simply stares out the window
where an old broken-down tractor stands

in the backyard, grass screaming out of
worn sprockets, joints rusting above slow
gulfs of shadow shot wild with foxglove.

The Wire Gang

Seasons slip and flow through jackalberry and wattle.
Veldt and rock glisten with the redolence of minerals
rising off dew. Savannah skies brighten. Rollers settle
on telephone lines, the thin shine stringing paddocks
out north where flat farmland undulates into blue hills
textured soft by the way the distant rural land looks.

By the time the grass is dry, a worn path runs along
the wire-line. Tobacco smoke accompanies the work –
thuds on earth and shunts of steel, the auger's song
screwing deep into the soil – hollowing out each hole.
Broken ground receives treated wood, creosote dark
on calloused hands piling in each staggered gum pole.

Beneath munhondo and stinkwood, bales of wire
gleam – sun-spat and charged. A sack of milled grain
stands beside an old billycan boiling over an open fire.
Men's shadows fall side by side with nature and labour –
the sun dictating the wire's ease, dawn's hard vein
softened beneath a sky offering the malleable pallor

afternoons endorse with heat. And when the slack line
is lifted – tension drawn pole to pole – rungs of flash-
lit staves sing along a bluish reel, the barbed shine
running miles, a song running deep into the horizon.
And men have died by the wire, the easy give of flesh,
the slip of a drawn force whistling with a final hymn

the soul must praise and resign to. But the gang work
on – the skill of faceless men working for the land's
gain. From sun-up to sunset, over savannah and rock,
the workforce strumming pole and steel, laying wire,
squaring acres off; each labourer's hardened hands
knowing nothing but work, a wife's skin, and prayer.

The Surgeon's Knot

He wades out a few feet where the current slows
to form fingered wash lines mingling into the pool.
His shadow bathed in gin water. Black fern and rock
asleep on the riverbed. Unaided, he struggles to work
the rod, whipping the fly through the air – bulrushes
wild with mating displays of bishops and widows,

red jewelled damselflies. The sun slowly reels left
over thick green forests hugging native hills. Clouds
of midges hover above mud banks like magic grain.
He savours the soothing views, the cool mountain
air lulling the pain he endures, the reel's white mercury
whistling wet above his head. With each fly swept

downstream, each spent thought rides the drifting
naturals, slipping into the current's glassy sinews.
Sun-snatched kisses draw him in deeper. The river
cold at his hip, the hypnotic depth haunted by silver
turns cut white with speed. Gaunt yet staid, he stands
sewn into a corner of the Gairezi – sedge-fly rising

gently off the film. There, he cuts the line and ties
another on, the hackled fly dark as the angled hook –
the line's tapered shine waiting for cupped threshes
to take the light. And there he waits, freckled flashes
of muscle twisting wild between rock and shadow,
the flexed light churning the shallows of his eyes.

In the Music of Labour

At first the stubborn growth resists him, till each stroke
is fluently flung to clear the knee-high grass, his task
down to an art, the pendulous swing of knees slightly
giving, his right arm catching the sun wet off the blade.

All day the work, shuffling steps into shuffled clearings,
beetles and crickets rising off cordite clicks sparking
off stone, bearded chin sequinned with sweat. The heat
seems not to bother him, but steels his concentration

deep in the trials of his faith. Why the sun rises and falls,
why his jaundiced wife believes God will save them all,
is just as unclear as why his newborn's unfinished death
hangs heavy on every dawn. In the music of his labour,

each composed thresh throws slashed grass to sunlight,
each mastered stroke floats timed beneath the weight
of the sun burning deep into his heart, the mastered art
of his arm fluent with the song the hours constantly sing.

At Measure

It's the dreamy air that will send you off to your death,
the dark silence stoking amber light in the distance.
And you're heading home, the car droning along at speed,
that safe speed that keeps your blood warm and cradles
your heart. Your foot's steady on the accelerator, every
peaceful thought you own kneels at the altar of your being.

Stars play accomplice to the magic of small villages,
neon lights hurtle by without sound – the names of towns
flung into the glass depth of your rear-view, where
everything vanishes. Fourteen hours straight at
the wheel, in three hours' time it will be her birthday;
you'll walk silently into the house, slip off your shoes,

climb the stairs, undress, then slide into bed with her.
You'll make love, and stay up till dawn embraced in the age-
old gesture. Through West Nicholson to Colleen Bawn,
the darkness parts for you, the car slips through time.
On the seat beside your own: a veined roadmap of South Africa,
a small velvet jewellery box, a bottle of warm red wine.

The Parlour

Light on his heels and proudly Rhodesian,
the professor pours each measure of gin like
an ace loving the sound of ice on glass.
Rainfall rings off roof tin – Virgil, the Alsatian,
snug asleep with Dante the Labrador; *Jesus!*
Fucking lazy bastards, snuggled together like
Siegfried & Roy, sniffing up each other's
arses! Large hairy balls thundering purple as
plums. Two boys, delicate young Audens,
lie sprawled on sofas with G&Ts, subscription
New Yorkers carelessly flung to the floor.
'Take your drink long or short?' – 'Depends
on the glass.' Then small talk about education,
the importance of poetry and the past – Taverner
in the background, twill damask drapes
falling from ornate brass railings, cherubs
on the ceiling frigging around God. Two grape-
blue lampshades, held by more naked cherubs,
stand in sweet smoky corners, white marble
skin grey in the warm-lidded air, work table
stacked high with books, walls all spines
and names. The professor groans, leans back
into his armchair, Peterson pipe cool, thumb
on bowl like a gavel ...*corrupt senators mine*
our lives for another war, he says, stamping black
ash on to the flat of his supine palm.

St Joseph's Fields

Again, the Ayres Thrush flips up then dives fast from
the sky, pale breast skimming over the row crop, white
mist sour off each wing before rising above blue gum;
the field shadowed by the windbreak's muscled height.
Nose up, and the craft banks left, the sky a summary
of dreams caught in a blue vault where each memory

lies anchored for a while then dissolves. Again, the low
flight buzzing over soy, the craft's paper-weight echo
lifting after the final run – the fine spray rolling slick
through broadleaf laid flat beneath the sun; blue gum
short off the craft's belly. Then, the sky's automatic
turn to the east, altitude locked above a gutted home-

stead where a pool's emerald glare throws sunlight
up like a polished jewel, torched outhouses cavernous
and bare. Two trailers lie jack-knifed beside a white
Bedford truck stripped back like a rotting cattle carcass.
From there, fields turn wild with grass – open vleis
spattered white with settlements of St Joseph lilies,

tall blooms bowing miles without a thought of town.
From the air the faint shadow of the craft is thrown
to the ground by a desolate sun, the plane a bird over
marshland, a bird flying through uncalculated freedom
where one incessant thought begins to pry another
with the wish to leave what was always known as home.

The Naming of a Child

It began with a leisured cycle of turning strokes,
every breath drawing on syllables, her name dug
from each jab stirring the brown muddy water.
An upward glance took in bare skies, corncrakes
weak on the wing, the slow evening light – slug-
silver. Stroke after stroke, warm turns of water
rippled back to quiet mud banks where plover
pressed banded breasts against the inverted sky.
The sun fell bald with thoughts of our daughter
swimming in your womb, her arms turning over
with mine till depth drew me to stop and look up
and hear nothing but starlight crowning the sky.
There, in the music, she was named, deep in the cup
of the agrestic valley where sound worships water
and flows into the cradle of every villager's arm,
the sweet consistency of life, expectant and warm.

Audition

This year's sun slips pale through monkey puzzle, the spiny branches
twisting their thin shadows above the old square engulfed by weeds.
A gazebo leans beside sagged benches, memories of packed lunches
hold strong: Creme Sodas, ginger beers, wet-nosed dogs tugging leads

over rainbow-fresh cranesbill, the lunch-hour sun warm as the dream.
And though Prince Edward Street still slings traffic out to Kensington,
Rowland Square lies dead asleep, the neglected park a lonely emblem
ravaged by a knotted plague, scabbed rosewood filtering out the sun.

Yet Milton Park hoists flags and emblazoned crests on adjacent lanes,
lanes with old English and Dutch names sophisticated with elision,
brass plates and numbers tagging private walls, hedged fences, lawns
pristine as verdant silk, pools of rich cool shade working the illusion.

Back in Rowland Square, hidden deep in a fold of the mottled road,
the elocutionist's house stands quietly forgotten, colonial and green.
On the letterbox, a cardboard sign: *Peanut butter for sale.* A toad-
stool and two weather-worn gnomes block the driveway. An engine

from a skiff, propped against the shell of a stripped Renault 6. Light
citrus smells whip through the heavy perfume of guavas. Somewhere
a voice calls, the wet wound of my name weeping in the dimpled light.
The kitchen stable-door slowly opens. A kettle's whistle thins the air.

★

> *So, imagine you're in a hall.*
> *Look at me! Centre yourself. Look at me.*
> *So imagine you're in a hall without a microphone.*
> *Breathe. Take a deep breath.*
>> *Read.*
> *Read with the whole hall watching.*
> *Read with every member listening.*
> *Centre yourself.*
>> *Focus. Read.*

An old typewriter lies on her desk, a sheet of words half engaged.
    A bouquet of medicines, bitter and fresh. A fifth of gin
pacifies a huge wooden carving of a Malaysian lion.
Wax polish and citrus oils linger over floors and sills.
    Births and deaths rest in teacups fired in ancient kilns.
        Leafs over china grains.
            Again!
    The dead knock of her cane.
Fear must never become boring.
    And some bullshit after that failing to hit the mark.
Some packaged crap for drama students that also works with CEOs
from local banks, and the occasional *liberal* wanker
        attached to an NGO.
            Again!

                        ★

The walk to the car is slow after hours working passed the first
                                milestone.
She says, *Come again. We'll work on diction and free your tongue.*
The sweep of her dragged foot follows the sweet knock of her cane.
Her glasses, round and 1980s, shouting over wild waves of hair flung
back over a worn knitted cardigan, the years flowing white off
                                every strand.
Hard to think of the girl before this woman, riding through Land's End,
pushing the horse hard, buttocks tight above the saddle, a fired youth
breaking speeds too wild to contain anything, even the thought of death.

                        ★

When a man emerges from a neighbouring driveway
with a sign: OPEN 5pm TILL LATE, she turns her head,
gently pushing her chin into her collarbone.
    Another man appears, Chinese lantern dangling from a pole,
a red whisper glowing in the evening shade;
the boughs of tulip trees, all dark muscle, growing fuller with each
laboured step.
    We stand by the car, discussing theatre and cinema,
over her shoulder, a bright new clinic shuts down for the day.
A man on a bicycle rides by and waves shyly −

her deep smile coupled by a girlish reaction:
perhaps a thought to jump and make a giddy wave when waving back.
                    But no, she turns, resuming her staccato way,

> *Don't forget. Practise every day.*
> *Be back next week.*
> *Let fear run freely through you.*
> *Fear keeps you alert.*
> > *But for fuck's sake,*
> *don't let it rule you.*

Evening shadows congeal, and the sky – for the first time in years –
seems a dome on which constellations fight in union to keep seasons
fixed on slippery charts.

A sense of grieving taints everything, the grief of a death
through malpractice: a crippled horse tethered like a goat, a badly
aimed shot blowing cheekbone and chin apart, the horse's muzzle
dangling loose with every vowel of recklessness wagging slack
beneath a bloodshot moon forelocked by the wind.

This memory still drags off her cane, her love of men
questioned. The rifle's shot blowing the dreamers' lantern out, over
and over.

Again.

★

We met when the season was cold,
            the wind slicing thin off the sun's edge.
Things then were sacrificed for less than now,
the world performed in constant audition for what would always happen.
            Our words drew strength from the dead,
        blank canvases burning a black mortal coil.
Here we were falling senselessly into a music without sound.
            Our lives scripted, knowing no defiance.

Kubvumbi

The shape of us builds faintly from sleeping hills,
the pale morning rain whispering her name. She holds
my finger, asleep, her warm grip tight and simple.
Neighbours wake to curse the weather, maize fields
sodden and dark. From dawn to dusk, the same grey
stare over the trudged hoof-suck of mud-trenched cattle
grieved by the trees. But here, the rhythm of drizzle
falls gently, filling our sleep with a layered peace,
our breaths shapeless, warm, enriched with a fortune
blossoming as the dawn begins to lay its wet light,
a shape growing strong, formed around our newborn.

The Dish

Stencilled on the mid–May evening sky, the relic stands –
avocado trees squatting below the bowl; iron belts and mesh
quietly gathering ancient starlight. Orion falls westward,
deep in the hunt – the heavens thick with fables, the rush
of white frequencies sluicing through air – babbled fronds
cradled in pockets of the expanding universe, the outward
     rush of an unknown wave burning bright with silica.

★

A dome of stars was language before the dish, the night sky
crisp with all its frequencies. Barefoot up on the roof, pole
and pool–net held high, coat–hangers attached to a wire led
to a radio. We searched night skies: arched backs locked to sole
and heel – our balance rooted to the roof, our ankles gently
flexed to turn our tender weight to a star where light bred
     language. First came Mozambique's stellar Portuguese.

★

The left arm reeled in, the right forced forth its quiet, clean
hydraulic movement – steady like a god moving an unthinkable
weight of air, a load of frequencies from Malawi to Russia
where poker–faced newsreaders followed game–shows. Unable
to grasp the various languages, things still held clear, the screen
spilling images captured by the dish, feeding out the picture
     of man. 1989, we watched how war began on C–SPAN.

★

Language, the shape of thought – the spark and black plug;
the sky needled with words and mathematics, the blueprint
of the universe ongoing with emotion, casual with every feat
we fail to fathom – the earth's soul our first and last point
of reference. Time can only translate our meaning, the flag
of reason black in our hearts, its dark language of fear: its heat
     burning bright off tongues with the death of stars.

★

To have known light translated life off this faint sound, every age
and every century another character deciphered, prophecies
reverberating back to the old world still steady in religion –
this was the dream heard by the lonely ear behind frequencies
undulating in unsteady tones on the dial. With this knowledge,
focusing upon stars bright in the heavens, the whispered radiation
　　　a lullaby in our bones, a song sung from the unknown.

★

Dishtowels dissolved on the clothesline beneath the antenna,
the moon's white sickle hung sharp above where rabbits huddled
in hutches; the terrified creatures delivered to small death boxes
children checked on by the day – each condemned creature loved
with fresh lettuces and carrots passed through wire mesh, sienna
stains on grass leading to a constant sermon of flies on black rocks
　　　where Bugs and his pals shat, their necks being wrung.

★

And to have the cooling light, the straw taut lawn, nocturnal
termites busy on winter's brittle ground, the hawk moths drawn
silent beneath the oil-filmed sky, deadlight slick on its surface,
mesh and steel rounding the ear of history above a khaki throne –
all mystery's wealth. A weaver's nest hangs alone – an ancient symbol
fading into the sky, a clot of birth reabsorbed from a race
　　　of thoughts sharing a genuine biology too close to link.

His Sunday Shift

The morning's sacred breath slants in through
small arched windows, the cold churchlike silence
sequinned with steel parting hide from warm flesh;
each stroke – clean, deliberate. Tapestries of blue
gossamer fold delicately over the ceiling, fresh
waves brightening to a white film – every sense

of death given to a quiet hunkered prayer rising
swiftly from hoof to neck and clod – the blade's
silver benediction. A bull's head rests on a concrete
altar staring at oiled swirls of blood screwing
down a drain, the stream slick beneath his feet.
An inner coolness lies still and wet. The outside

stench draws blowflies thick behind the gauze;
by noon the gauze rings black with flight. Time
is all hook and pulley. The red, marbled vestments
of slaughter raw off the bone saw's jagged gaze,
the worn folds of the teenager's priestly garments
stained with the incense of burnt alum and lime.

And Evenings Come Like This...

Dry toothless gears keep the donkeys' hours,
the bored well's stutter churning gold in pails.
Not one word from the other women, all sour-
faced as she knelt to take her turn – cowbells
pealing out beyond scythed fields where songs
were sung over open fires till dawn, the grave-
site heaped with upturned earth. He was young,
seven or so, emaciated, barely able to drive
cattle when they drove him out into the field
where death swooped upon him with no trouble.
Now evenings come like this, trees stencilled
on the sky, donkeys at their pace at the wheel.
She stands, water spilling from the pail, turns
and walks away to the empty hut where her son
would wake to hear her troubled breath burn
beneath the hot snatched curses of other men.

Engine Philosophers

The smell of steel and oil is the incense of our labour.
    In fields shot green with growth, brittle with grain,
or bare as anvils – we extend our hands over the iron altar.
Sometimes visions are lost through the slip of a spanner,
    a misplaced nut collapses a thought like a faulty jack.
But no real workman worth his salt jumps in straight off the bat
to rotate a shaft or turn a bolt. Down to changing a wheel,
a moment's silence honours an established principle.

Tractors, trailers, bowsers and sumps, planters, gauges,
    hydraulic pumps worked by drivers of different ages,
from different owners of different sexes, all contribute in sync
to at least three Arcadian laws governing modern mechanics.
    Sweet milky tea does the rounds. Discourse begins.
Here is where the poses of hands-in-pockets and fists-on-chins
perfected the way a solemn frown holds a solemn thought.
Here real thinkers never smear oil, from worked engines,

between thumb and forefinger; that's just not done
    beneath galvanised roofs of workshops or the bare
punishing slap of the sun. Not real thinkers! Something European
makes us want to speak German. And through the common
    phrase about all knowledge being interpretation –
cogwheels and chains turn in our heads. Consideration
changes down to movement. Old tools of knowledge, worked
and scarred, gleam flatly with the nature of honest work.

Cirrus

The time has come now when there's nothing
to talk about, the horizon home terribly beautiful,
even in old age your silence is bolted and strong.
Loose clothes mock your health with cold simplicity:
your blouse sloped to the left, revealing a bare
atoll of bone. A pair of loved shoes refuses to hold
your feet – when you walk they suck at your heels
        as you drag your handbag.

So what of these mares' tails, these cirrus whips
above – masses of cloud on fire in the western skies,
these ships waiting, the wisps of sirens playing
backward from their burning decks, a terrible reversal
        – the lick-back of beautiful things.

Maize fields stand tall. The dusk light blinds
the way home as though the matron of your ward
(all soft-spoken but firm, grey garb and breast watch)
ordered the sky to cloak all worry. Silence is not simple,
the road, almost a ritual passage to an evening
        descending on you with a passionate fear.

Copper Fall

After the goshawk and gymnogene take to the sky and roost,
the ample leisure of sunlight falls red on a breeze turning over
buried paths – treasured compost underfoot, warm and soft –
a dark secret wet with millipedes and termites. The sky fades
with the delicate vowels of birds ringing down muscular hills,
streams carving contours through green valleys, the sunset
flattening fast to white layers of mist where prayers of leaves
slip through sacred air; the evening tanned with a copper veil –
the forest thick beneath the moon rusting above sleeping hills.

Nagapie

Bean-chaff and husk scuttle over gravel
polished blue by the wind's electric confessions,
    soy fields bare beneath dry constellations
        burning bright with sharp breaths of frost.

And the nagapie screams through tangled
limbs of cypresses, her breath flung beyond
    the wrought iron fence where the ground
        breeds barbs spiked with beads of red dew.

A slow naked sun drags the morning in,
shrikes whistle and prance on thirsty lawns, louries
    call through guava trees while vervet monkeys
        squall and fight over the fruit of the sycamore fig,

the mulberries all gone. Seasoned cattle
change in temperament, the cold nights hardening
    their gaze on the ground where short fattening
        grasses thin out as pastures bald with the sun

leaning into quiet shadows; nothing else
but this succession of light where thoughts lie lost
    in candlelit dreams, the dark scream of ghosts
        sung wild off the moon's charred, white breath.

VHS

It's a strange thing watching a dead man's wedding,
but we cracked open the beers, feet up on the table –
     adjusting the volume with the remote control.
       The film begins with a bang!
The groom *pussy-licking* the air, flicking his tongue,
pulling the finger before palming the lens black.
His muffled laugh lingers. The blank screen leers back.

Annoyed by the camera's presence, a nervous bride
buries her head in busy arms adding finishing touches
     to her hair. A voice off screen: the bride blushes
       and smiles at the camera –
the shot over her shoulder catching a girl in the mirror
modelling gloves too large to fit her hands, wearing
a veil pristine and white as the stone on the bride's ring.

Alternating scenes lead to a take of one steady shot:
red aisle, small acoustic church, walls thick as a tomb's,
     father and bride slowly walking to the groom.
       Scriptures read. Vows spoken.
A shy impassioned kiss sets the whole congregation
alight with whooping chants for more, this time: *Firm
with tongue action!* The tape shudders, warping the film.

The reception bit is grainy: the best man's speech,
the cake, the newlyweds' first dance with parents unsure
     of the music, a scuffle for flowers on the floor…
       In a line-out, men pissed on beer
elbow each other for the garter. Then, from nowhere,
the wedded pair in a parking-lot barking a roll of thanks,
eighties music in the background. The groom wanks

off a suggested boredom, feigning a laboured yawn,
till a man's embrace draws them close, the man's face
    lost in hurried kisses, port or wine spilt on lace,
        a bearded laugh, reading glasses
blindingly bright with clumsy lighting. Perhaps a notorious
uncle always pissed, a family friend the couple knew...
The filmmaker's mark blots the end like a botched tattoo.

State House

A light after-sense of *Fleurissimo* haunts the air,
the velvet sun shunting through passage windows,
polished brass twists light elegantly everywhere.
Door to door, the corridor's carpet sucks in every
footstep, a deep yet fleeting anticipation set below
the roll of heel and sole. You can hear them behind
the door, the soft churning murmurs, the pale ivory
walls cradling light and sound. A white gloved hand
turns the handle just short of my chest – the door
opening to a simple room, white linen, naked floor.
A manservant in colonial whites pulls out a chair.
A bell rings, the lidded perfume heavy on the air.

The Wheel Brace

Both men spat red dirt, the tractors' engines echoing off cypress
windbreaks smudged silver with heat – gears, shafts and star-wheels
circling raw motion into windrows. Dust steamed off mown grass,
fields stripped back with lizards and mice darting beneath kestrels

locked to the sky. Distant thunder drummed its black murderous
roll – diesel plumes floating thick above the spot where the drivers
stopped, disembarked and went for each other beneath the ulcerous
sky. Next morning a constable was called. At the stables mourners

stared into red earth – the blue sky drilled clean with a white sun.
Out in the field, a tractor and baler ran jettisoning bales lashed taut
with twine, the tractor simply swerving over ground where the iron
bar had been found, ruby wet with dew, where the men had fought.

Moonflowers

With bush fires the wind woke to rise,
breathing through the southern skies –
the air sweeping white over fields of
silent legumes. A stillness rose above

the rural balance, carving cemeteries
out of villages pregnant with bodies
buried beneath nameless crucifixes of
wood. What death could not remove

lay startled, waiting to be carted away.
Feasting bats tumbled through insects,
the cold crammed skies dark as tombs,

thin silk petals falling red as the moon
rose over each village sick with secrets,
the wind gone with the full light of day.

Gleaners

The earth's canvas has them bending over in stubble fields.
    Their hips – axles of labour – shadows doubled above
the worked ground. Shrivelled sacks build slightly by the hour.
Iron hoes, stacked among sheaves, collect the sun's heat –
    burning with flashing speed, opening up vermin's nests.

Whole families work in teams, spaced out across flat acres;
    and nowadays bicycles park on barbed-wire fences –
while far infield women straighten to speak on phones,
    swaddled children sweating fast asleep on their backs.

Ironwood and gum stifle vortices of dust. Rural roads
    spray frayed ribbons around fields throwing maize husks
        to religious heights of secretary birds:
Up, up to the view where the land below becomes geometry,
where fields are quadrangles beside perfect circles,

where belts of shine slither into blue tri-angled dams.
    And with animated time-lapse progression,
the fields are gleaned beneath a weak sun falling rust quiet,
before farmland reawakens under the harnessed run of engines
    trailed by bright colours of agricultural graphs.

At the Work Yard

As Big-Boy-Sixteen and Canteen stood straining
to pull the borehole pump up – pulley and chain –
the tractor came screaming in: Pension struggling
to find the words – something about Sixpence
and the welding machine, the cold sun falling flat
on Pension's blood-spattered overalls, Innocence

wide-eyed by the tractor, face like a thief's caught
in a spotlight. At the work yard, pools of blood
had quickly turned black on the sand. A wrought
iron rod stood stubborn on a broken cultivation disc,
the rod slanted like a style on a sundial. Boot heels
carved tramlines in the sand leading to the kiosk

where Sixpence sat hunched in the laboured sound
of his own breath; each guttural wheeze weakening
with sighs, ribs ridged by the sun – skin browned
by an unspoken lineage. As blood caked at his feet,
Deliverance placed his palm to Sixpence's forehead
and prayed, the blood at his heels turning to concrete.

A Pale View of Citrus Fields

By some mistake he had woken to the truth
of what was actually happening. His father
dead, his mistress back with her husband
working out their marriage – his daughter
in the city living with the nuns. His hands
trembled, the cool sun grey on his fingernails.
He'd said a lot of things, not knowing their
true meaning. Pockets of firefinch and waxbills
coloured the brown brittle lawn, the dry air
wild with birdsong. For five years he'd slept
with a pistol under his pillow, his mattress
grooved with the gun's heavy shape. He kept
the safety off at all times. After he got dressed,
he sat on the verandah, had scrambled eggs
with champagne, read the paper off the net
while bulbuls busied about him picking insects
at his feet, the bulb above his head still hot
with light, his thoughts fading into his youth.

Barely Sixteen

Each workman will gladly squander his time,
place the spade to rest, lean on a rake or hoe.
Tractor drivers know dead on at six she'll pass
the work yard, to and fro, the sun each time
pressed up against the land, rising or sinking.

Naturally aware, there's sex in every stride;
her tall frame, wide mouth, thick plaited hair.
Always an element of bare skin in the art of
walking, her naked back, uncurtained thigh,
the sun warm against the land, rising, sinking.

Candle Thorn

Goatsuckers and spotted dikkop fell silent. Night
sky black without a single star. Wind polished
for sound. When the car came tearing up the drive –
horn blaring, headlights branding the gridiron gate –
something set him steadfast to his place, something
held him back to let the dead do their own dying.
Then and there, every code of solidarity vanished
with one simple reason driving him to stay alive.

Time drew on. Dust rose like steam on fire. Trees
hunched naked over the horn piercing the dirt-dry air.
He held back. Nostrils flared. Heat from his lungs
falling back to sniffles stifled over huddled knees.
Before the car, distant gunfire rang out – clasped
bursts locking down the flat commercial landscape,
the cold shape of fate cradled in the arms of prayer.
Then silence, black as the barrelled steel he clung

to, buttstock pressed into his shoulder, breeze
parting the drapes with a whisper. The headlights
drew back, fading behind him, fast off a bare wall
where four pudgy faces dissolved like pills. The breeze
fell thin. Darkness settled thick on the verandah.
The pick-up tore down the dirt strip, black thunder
billowing out in its wake – bright red tail-lights
vanishing like hot coals thrown down a dirty well.

A Faith

In fields along all roads leading to Jerusalem,
the bald and barefooted pray beneath the halo
of a cracked sun, every heel's naked shadow
staining the baked ground. Here, biblical times

still reign over the lives of educated women,
daughters' dreams thrown to baying shadows
drawn by lust, turning wives to mothers below
the age of consent, all this through religion –

knees rooted to dust in the stance of worship.
Along all roads leading to cities and townships,
white robes gather in fields where innocence

surrenders its feathered weight – the lauded
hands of prophets hovering above bald-headed
girls primed to serve desire's omnipotence.

Tobacco Country

With each tier-pole drawn from the barn, the silhouettes
marched into the grading-shed, shoulder to neck,
    linked by heat-stained steel.

Two foremen with sjamboks barked behind the gang,
winter's clasp tight on each labourer's ankle,
    chains of red fog dragging

the evening at swollen heels. After nightfall, the men
were led into the barn like ghosts stepping onto
    a boat leaving the continent –

each death linked by nothing else but the promise of work.
Fuck leaving a gap! said the one foreman,
    There's tons of air…

So in they went to settle, the warm drone of the coal-fan
drugging the labourers to sleep, moonlight spilling
    bright over pink flowered fields.

Oxbow

Quiet on the wing, a pearled rush of pochard gaze on trout
turning fat on wishing stars, the evening air running briskly
through guinea grass hazed pink with the coming drought.
Waterbuck draw in, all ghostlike, genuflecting to kiss a sky
wild with constellations – wide nostrils flared with thunder,
    polished hooves drumming the rock-rubble of the valley.

The wind gently eases back into the night's quiet surrender,
water mirroring the moon's white horns. Solitude gradually
suggests a need for human company, the sky's salted ceiling
sprayed above ambling hills. Embers pulse with a slow art,
each amber hour cradled then hurled off time's elastic sling,
    the ancient silence hurling stars deep into the river's heart.

Amnesia

Mimosa comes alive with chatter, dusk's reverse
manner trumpeted by cockerels. Children's laughter
surges, folding silk red shrouds of dust over a game
of football. Nearby, goats stand on a trough sipping
water – the backdrop: a fallow field with the silhouette
of an old green engine, the sun hauling amnesia in.

Men with heavy heads and greased overalls walk past
like ghosts to cramped houses fucked with smoke.
Saturday's done, a gallon of sun dumbs wives' screams,
wives praying for the fresh dawn walks their children
take into fog-layered fields, singing songs through
gilded sheets of sunlight – the walk to Bryn Farm

for school. But now the goalposts of rapoko stalks
defy all natural laws and stand. Instinctively the goats
make their way to the pens. The sun sets. All that's left
on the horizon – hazed silhouettes of children being
swallowed whole, their laughter subsiding, a red
bruise turning black fast where the sun went down.

Portrait off a Water Trough

It was here the old man drank and wiped his mouth,
cupped the cool water and bathed his face with a deep
exhale – his smooth balding scalp shining beneath
the sun like polished soapstone. The day had been long,
the search forlorn, whistling and clicking his tongue,
a small sack of boiled sweet potatoes slung back over

his shoulder, bamboo cane sifting through lovegrass.
He'd walked with the rising sun – whistling, clicking,
his gait limp and slow, the blond expanse glistening
off boots rugged with repair. But where was the calf
he sought? The calf's mother suckling on her own teat
back in the maternity pen, egrets white on the fence.

To be born in 1931 means nothing here – joints ache
with each tired step, only the sky and rural landscape
soothe the memory's walk deep with the quiet intake
of death. The wind sings through the grass, parrots rise
from bare trees, yet youth still whispers some reprise
his hunched shadow won't easily surrender or forget.

He knows the calf lies somewhere low and searches
for shallow disturbances, a thermal of jackal buzzards
soars west off the reclining sun, shattered skull-gourds
of wild oranges littering the bush. He walks to where
the windmill turns its sweet exercise, the steady gleam
of silver blades levelling the trough to a simple mirror;

and here the old man stops and drinks, the full moon
rising where the sun rose, the sun steadily sinking into
the horizon. And for a while he stands still, the June
air quickly turning cold, the broken look of a stranger,
toothless and bald, staring back off wrinkled water
his hands left to settle, the sky nailed wet with stars.

The Coucal and the Smoker

Her moss-glossed, chestnut flight shadows parsley,
the cool garden air settling into silver layered depths
reaching out over turnips swollen at the root. Celery
stalks stand taut, ribbed with sodium. Hawk moths
shift and hover above hedges of flowering lavender,
      the seasoning of eastern stars coating silhouettes

with a fine saffron line. Pale cauliflower curds rest
fat like simple minds in-rowed with bladed chives;
pumpkin leaves relax and breathe beside coriander
bathed in crisp bouquets of freshly baled grass –
each bale pressed against wrought iron fence-posts
      bent deep by bulls sparring in the cartwheel's hub.

Fig leaves crack underfoot where Langstroth hives
stir beneath a milk-stoked moonlight, bellowed notes
singing weak off the hum of bees, each sweet brass
wedge set to pails beside fennel-flavoured beds; herb
and life, air and nature glowing slow beneath a task
      sung heavy with the golden harvest of smoke.

Gates of Dawn

For this is the last best gift that the kindly demigod is careful to bestow on those
to whom he has revealed himself in their helping: the gift of forgetfulness. Lest the
awful remembrance should remain and grow, and overshadow mirth and pleasure,
and the great haunting memory should spoil the afterlives of little animals helped
out of difficulties, in order that they should be happy and light-hearted as before.
                                    – Kenneth Grahame, *The Wind in the Willows*

Twenty years or more passed since I last saw this man
standing here, mirroring my shock. Still short, Ralph stands
with the same pronounced forehead from schooldays
when we called him Rat, partly because of his front teeth,
partly through the need of a name. Lost in the maze
of a hidden world, we watched each year simmer beneath
muscled shadows of towering trees, where every episode
of youth turned black in the *Back Woods*. Carl was Toad,
I was Mole, and Arden – simply for his sheer size –
was Badger: grand, old, invincible. But Arden wasn't wise
and Ralph never occupied himself with the *mutterings*
            or writings of poetry things.

                              ★

Day after day blackouts black the nights. On the streets
long queues stretch thin – curling back on cold concrete
sidewalks warming up beneath the morning sun. People
read the papers, some sit staring lost in thoughts other
minds refuse to engage. Headlines play into the sequel
of cruel endless days beneath the state's burning banner.
Babies on mothers' backs cry. Men smoke crude
cigarettes. Sometimes an explosion of laughter after a rude
joke about the government. Here strangers need not ask
what works or fucks things up – this comedy of an axe
thrown blindly into the arsehole of history by History.
            Race and power rotating on the axes of money.

                              ★

Champagne-white and fast, a Clio speeds past. A teenager
head and shoulders out the window – salutes the finger,
pumps his fist, shouting wildly, ...*the call must be for us!*
No-one knows what he was on about. For a while a bemused
silence rings before elders comment on the state of urban youths.
Young mothers refresh domestic issues, every dull topic abused
on local TV shows. Men shake their heads – their laughter
burning deep within souls raging wild with fire, a laughter
reversed – dark as echoes of grief flowering on every lapel.
Across the road, dignitaries exit taxis to enter the hotel –
the sun reflecting blindly off thick mirrored doors, hot rays
       flashing bright, forcing heads to turn away.

          ★

Ralph sets down two rolled canvases to take my number.
Says we must meet before he heads off to Edinburgh –
A beer at The Keg. Seeing himself as a painter, he laughs
with a snort. Says Carl's in Dubai flying the royal family,
Still a bachelor. Fucking all those expat women in the Gulf!
Winks. Smiles. Cunningly reiterates the word '*Gulf*'; finally –
a glimpse of the old boy. But no one knows where Badger is,
some established silences remain. And as Ralph keys in
my name, the wilderness of rocks and trees returns;
our band of four, hands black – soiled with juice wrung
from hibiscus stalks, sticky earth moulded onto blind roots,
       dirt grenades swung to bamboo forts

occupied by Latin scholars primed with mathematics.
It all came back: running battles, socks spiked with blackjacks,
Arden swinging a boy by the legs, damp smells of earth,
rocks tattooed with lichen; the fear spokes of golden lyres,
the golden orbs' neat long furred tentacles black with death
glistening in the guarded sunlight. Here the world's fires
of dream and fantasy burned with a eudaimonic violence;
known, unknown things, entering secrecy without grievance,
every fable challenging truth with youth springing forth
for the Piper to wait on the sweet mysteries of death,
where stoats guarded weasels and ferrets by their own law,
       laying task to claim any task laid for war.

That the fort became our world became the essential tool,
longing for the rocks – sitting bored in the back rows, school
lunch sedating us, boreworst and chips, the *Back Woods*
calling, the Piper's sweet needling flute drawing us to nod
deep into a sparkle where panic raised its jewelled hood
with its black imperious summons, the angered demigod
hypnotically licking time off every sweet layer of the sun
till the brass bell woke us with the gong of its lobed tongue.
A primal wire fired through our blood, a vengeance-spark
red with disorder, the call to the rooted rocks – dark
in its weight and desire, the sole of our naked purpose
      flat with the gait of avarice. Void of remorse.

★

Ralph's thumb pecks the keys on his phone. My hand on
his shoulder. Champagne Clio long gone. The morning sun
lumbering above the city, forcing short shadows to squat
thick at the foot of their shapes, the heat at work on the tar,
the city's streets slow and soft with submission. And that
was it, the mist of every year unveiled, our history, far
from done with this comedy, far from done with its misery
lodged deep within every heart, the simple art of tragedy
sweet on every dawn. *'Rat!' he found breath to whisper,*
shaking. 'Are you afraid?' 'Afraid?' murmured
the Rat, his eyes shining with unutterable love. 'Afraid!
Of Him? O, never, never! And yet – O, Mole, I am afraid!'

Hunters' Society

Evening falls to the contrabass of bullfrogs,
the velvet musk of Davidoff and Calvados
faint behind his back. Those who had come

out for the sunset stood watching the brass
white moon rise above the grand hypnotic
veldt; the waterhole pewter-still, wild plum

on the banks. He breathed in the heavy air
and thought how he had travelled the world
to lose his mind in such untamed country.

A shadow on the water rippled out in circles.
Gun oils railed off teak. The old belvedere
glowing weak, a soft flame in a lost century.

A Place for a Windmill

Barefoot, he strides through warm religious
light, the sun crowning his outstretched arm.
Where a rock cairn stands, he slows – glass
and light trembling, the tumbler on his palm
drawn to the ground, spilling wet light to earth.
Again, same thing three times over, the rite
of water and soil unfolding where the earth
draws heavy on water's blind desire for light.

A zephyr curls, lifting maize husks and dust
over a scotch-cart loaded with tools. Shovels
and pickaxes flash fresh with effort – the rust-
red depth dulling steel, the grate of wet gravel
sweetening the ear for the splash of shadows
to crown the sun with unburdened applause.

Easygoing

The mention of Catholics leaves a dirty look
on most of their faces, *For here is where
God is simply God*, the Bible a reference book
chronicling people living in and out of prayer.
Where altars traditionally stand, a Suzuki keyboard
lays simple chords over slow sober rhythms
of a bass guitar. Photographs of rivers with words
of hymns flow fresh over stone – Pentecostal hymns –
arms thrown to heaven, hands open – swaying
in praise. Pastor Ray freely uses words like *shit*;
makes no bones about his sex life – saying
how sometimes it works, sometimes it doesn't,
*'...but the Lord knows how I love to fuck my wife,
how she loves to be fucked by me.'* So it goes down
easy with the congregation when this real life
preacher calls Herod a *cunt* during the sermon.
Not one gasp – just loud, frenzied hallelujahs
followed by *Amen!* After the service, friendly
wives in floral dresses serve tea in the foyer,
solemn men stand proud, the sun falling gently
on children at play. So this is it, a small harmless
sect on the outskirts of a northern suburb
going easily about its ways – hard to miss
the heavy smiles, the weary eye's subtle throb,
the strain of every breath released on Sundays.
So breathe, though nothing goes away; the sun
perfumes the lawn as casual talk after praise
eases thoughts we must all learn to abandon.

Gunyana

The old Rottweil's cough sent egrets squalling off
the old dairy roof. Beside a rusted milk machine,
a rinkhals twisted and hissed, the snake blown clean
in half, both muscled knots resigning beside a stiff

hen – the hen's salt white breast soaking up a lake
of blood and yolk. That year pale skies rained sour
with ash, for weeks the black feathered downpour
fell slow like twisted wire in a dream, the raw ache

of the land seared by wind over wounded paddocks;
curled spines, harped ribcages scattered amid rocks
speckled black with flies. Meat and honey bees

drew in each day's infernal summary: cicada choirs
screaming on the horizon, the horizon red with trees
clutching wild at the sky, the sky seared of any stars.

Daughters of Our Age

A few of the children smiled back, moulding water
and soil in the yard – leaving mud-phones to bake
in the sun; circles and squares on each tablet's face,
thick grass aerials plucked from a field nearby. After
lunch we watched a girl, posed as an adult, take
an incoming call, one arm gesturing over a grimace
to the sky – news of another family death. No tears
running down her face – her features clean of any
other expression but that raw, rigid, troubled stare
to the sky. More phones rang, and more mahogany
arms rose, reaching out to pluck the sun from the air.

Savannah Chapel

We'd buried our dead knowing women sucked cock
for a loaf of bread or a dirty dollar bill in the city, but here
the barbershop quartet jazzed up songs by Sam Cooke
and Al Green, the onyx sky folding over a thousand acres
of scrubland – evening oils weeping on the flat horizon.
Arm in arm, boaters and Ascot hats, the congregation
took to seats on bales lined as pews – the pearled flair

of expensive perfumes drifting softly over zebra aloe.
Now and then a safari truck dropped off a small party.
Elderly couples, from the trophy lounge, stood partly
lost before being led to chairs – their backs sinking low
into the rounded comfort of velvet sofas made to cradle
the carapace of old age. Bored teenage girls took slow
sure steps to ogle cars that shone like modern miracles,

the clean, bright angles parked where stubborn grass
and bush tomatoes fought disc and harrow to become
a curious parking lot; flat crowns dotted squat across
the golden landscape. Bridesmaids and the groom's
men walked circles, studying the earth in brand-new
shoes they'd never wear again. Restless children threw
tantrums, fenced with sticks – simply testing the sum

of their mothers' patience – who dusted off suits tight
at the seams, spat on thumbs to wipe their children's
faces clean. Then, with a fluidity achieved in dreams,
the reverend raised his hand, the quartet fell to a light
melodious hum, the air thinned and the sky turned pale
to mother-of-pearl. Roosting birds settled from flight,
a dust-driven breeze slithered lazily through the bales.

The congregation settled and straightened their backs.
Sharp-eyed parents admonished children with a glance
before gasps from the back rows fired a collective climax
sparked by the groom and guides riding in on elephants;
behind the groom, a horse-drawn carriage. The spectacle
conjured mixed measures of awe; the closer they got, people
stepped back from their seats. Suspicious of chance,

and ill at ease, others eyed their cars and thumbed their keys;
but most, most were lost to the almighty magnificence
of the beasts. And as though to further pronounce
our disbelief, the ground trembled... At the altar's crease
seven elephants knelt to spontaneous dance and song.
Women rolled ululate tongues. One man rose from his knees
in tears and said, *Perhaps the funeral days are gone.*

And from this utterance, all the joy of love returned
with such wild, unbridled flamboyance. Promised
steps drawing us along, promised hand to promised hand,
a different future fresh and kept from our jaundiced
views. It's true, we'd walked through something dark;
and though the sun set like a weeping wound, the stark
nature of our joy drew us up, and almost embarrassed us.

The Fig-route

Silver spike and foxtail fell thin off the causeway's
banks, the ground snake-lashed with dirty S's; foot-
prints and cloven spoor circling the soakaway's
edge – all the fields running east: fallow, sifted grey

with ash. In the pit, walled with brick and gravel,
a full-term goat cried deep in the throat of the well –
each curdled call echoed, drawing the doe deeper;
the well's mouth glistening wet. Our shadows fell

dark with burning crowns, black like the heralds
of death staring down at the dull white folds of hair
caught above the water's algae eye; the emerald
air thick with dead vermin. The doe's eyes rolled

back, shudder-shocked in blank folds of defeat,
one hind hoof thrown up unnaturally. At our feet:
a noose, a spade and crook kept silent company
like sleeping fools. A tarpaulin. A plastic bucket

cradling a Bowie knife. Sunlight bounced hard
up off the ground, wild fermented fruit sweetening
the heat. From black paddocks, where a fireguard
once ran its harrowed pleats beside a boulevard

of fig trees, the goat's tribe trotted in – grey dust
rising, folding like an ash-flag trailing at half mast.
Deep in the throes of birth, the doe yelled, her
cries echoing thinly beneath the glistening crust,

each breath drawing the doe deeper and deeper
to where the pit opened and glared, until its stone-
wet stare was paid with two splashed whispers:
the first whispered flat, the second much deeper.

On the Balcony

Standing there, staring back over Borrowdale Brook,
broad fairways ambling to lily pad greens. It took
less than three months for the bronze mask of death
to cool and hug his face, for his last laboured breath
to breathe. His nephew sits alone, schoolbooks

scattered over the dining table, an empty look
screwed to the teenager's face, the maid's white doek
descending dark spiral stairs. And he thinks of death
              standing there, staring back

over the golf course bright with houses in the brook,
listening to his sister's breaths heave and unhook
with pain as she suddenly says, *'His fuckin' fiftieth
was next year.'* And their mother's prolonged death
revisits them, the wraith white-eyed with shock,
              standing there, staring back…

A Killing

It took almost thirty minutes to herd the bulls
into the kraal. The sun blazing off their hides,
all black, burnished, unmarked sculpted muscle.
Their dark eyes shone, their muzzles glistening,
refusing the dry pallor of blond dust rising
from the ground – the earth's mist dissolving
somewhere above polished sickles of horns.
For a while the dance of shadows and death –
hooves drumming into a mad chaotic ground,
a frayed, careless rope flung like a dirty halo.

Some cowboy-playing man, swinging his hips
for a laugh, swung the lariat again. Onlookers
bowing with laughter missed the fluke catch.
The rope gripped. With each movement came
a refusal tightening at the base of the bull's
horns. Six men fought a tug-of-war for another
fifteen minutes. Cracked feet grated baked earth.
Bellows and pure force reared in disagreement –
to the rope, to the crowd, to the man standing
by a car wearing overalls, holding a simple axe.

On Sunday Mornings

walk down and enter history,
smoke white breeze over trilby
shadow, warm September air.
Corrugated roofs skirt over
iron railings, linking sunlight
store to store. Avenues run
wide as riverbeds cut straight,
ironed flat by the wind, sun
and rain. With the glare it's
almost a dated photograph
from 1922, stiff grey streets,
the growing town dwarfed
by the thought of surrounding
land, distant hills bounding
north. Now bitumen stands
thick where dark grit sands
absorbed sunlight, shaded
gables shrinking into heat,
old colonial names – faded
but blocked out in concrete –
speak like scripts on graves,
and not one car in sight, nor
a lone hum, but rustling leaves
scuttling by to a chorus caw
of crows, the town deep in
slumber, its people locked in
dreams they hardly remember
when they wake past noon –
the dry mists of September
turning through the small town.

Family Portrait

Proudly posed in Sunday bests beneath glass almost bulletproof,
husband smiles, faithful wife on the left, surrounded by youths
too square-faced and fat to be cut from a different cloth –
a good measure of defiance in the youngest daughter's eyes,
  Look at us you munts, we fuckin' existed!

The mantelpiece stands flush with silver, a late-nineteenth-century
mirror holds rust-speckled glass – a stack of gilded crockery
sleeps above a fireplace packed with wood. Squat ivory
tankards, etched with the names *Ambrose* and *Marge*,
  flank the dated photograph like baobab trunks.

But Marge is dead. Ambrose too. Both their sons creeping into
a mistrust fuelled by the news, middle age and certain views;
how the years came to fall so fast with lives falling through
a troubled inheritance, daughter sunk beneath the glass,
  deep beneath her own troubled existence.

Empress Mine

The drive would not take long to where she'd die;
      six months of pain bullying her quiet surrender.
Hunched with age, unable to stand, she sat by the fire
burdened with pots outside her son's house.

      Five weeks' wages to Empress Mine,
the town easily missed heading west from Venice
to Gokwe, the trees alight, fire-red, white-lime –
every stone along the route a sun-hit gem.

The Munyati runs low, men on bare black rocks
      with fishing poles hoist invisible flags,
sun-hardened women on all fours put their backs
into working froth from cheap soap, the spawn floating

      down the river's knuckled banks.
From there on, another bridge, then small buildings
stained reddish brown by sand, people standing
slumped and flat, their putty shadows warped by the sun.

A rural bus, jacked-up precariously, flaunts three
      missing wheels beside black conical mounds
fenced with a latticed gleam, a bright angled memory
of a working hell sparkling with the refuse of nickel.

      Here, the road to her village eludes her,
nothing clear after sixty years, each turn-off guessed,
each road worse than the one before – fissured
by rain, time running deep through each crack.

For her send-off to the village near the mine,
      children down the line to great-grandchildren
stood out and waved. Workers' wives with children
on their backs wished to come along for the drive,

      the midwife's eyes clouded with cataracts
ringed with years. With all the weeping done,
she sat packed in the back with her belongings, sisal sacks
and cardboard boxes beside an elderly daughter

who'd never known her mother's home. So we began;
      children chasing the car, laughter
drowning in thick tunnels of dust. The sun
at work on gleaned fields. The shiver of a cattle grid

      introduced the drone of bitumen on wheels.
Along the miles, gusts threw lost decades, trees
stood in tribute, waving old and new leaves,
the road reversing every breath in a sparkle of hours.

Gumiguru

I

The blue prophet blazed in the morning heat – perching silently on the fir-tree. Omen. If not omen – omega of death: the starling, stationed on the tree's top.

Rose bushes bloomed a week before, their furled petals darkening at the edges. The rain-gauge empty and webbed with tight blades of grass at its foot. Bees hovered above the lawn carpeted with jacaranda flowers. Sweet alyssum and lobelia hung in the warm shade of eaves – the baskets dripping around the house. Wasps took flight – building nests, while bulbuls swooped down, hawking insects as trees stood in the heat, waiting for the wind to blow. Each warm draught like the pant of a dog.

★

Tractor sound; hoarse diesel groans building up to the homestead. The drivers coming in for lunch, vehicles parking in shaded lots behind the sheds. Their bulk hauling up dust, the clangour of plough discs coated red with earth – exhaust fumes coughing up towers of thick cloud.

For the few minutes it took the procession to dock, the whole yard became an industrial cacophony of engine noise: the pulling-in, the revs, the shouts of drivers on their way to lunch.

And father slept through it all – curled in bed like an ancient fossil.

The starling keeping vigil.

★

How harsh the acacia field looked to the east: a lime-green forest of thorns in contrast to the distant harrowed fields. The short needle-leafed trees dominated the landscape, held no shadows – just a cruel hallucinatory effect of water flowing into a distance of dry heat.

Clumps of the hardy trees mottled the view from the window, as I looked out – past the cattle dip where my brother and I stared into the dark foetid water skinned with thick slime and dung. Past the kraal where cattle were held, then herded single file into the treated trough, where splashes of muck were coughed up on both sides: muscle struggling through the dark oil-coloured water – liquid spurting out – the beasts' bellows churning out for miles. Past the fig-tree where we found a goat's body, a makeshift spear in its belly, nipples shrivelled hard in the dusty heat – mouth open in a yawn, revealing its brown teeth and cracked, dark tongue. There, where we vowed never to go again, where anthills towered like orange castles of blood, where light fled quick when night encroached. That place, that mysterious place that caught my eye and held our fear. The wooden spear strung white with beads, decorated red and black with cloth.

II

Where wind gave life was a sparkle in a field, a glint of blades turning, and up close – the great sound of metal rolling, chopping up air. And water, the cool sound of clear water, splashing into the reservoir, belts of shimmer dancing up – dreamily lashing white breasts of egrets perched on its edge.

He stood, broad-brimmed hat and khaki shorts, one hand on its metal frame. Four years after the rise of the new flag, the country still warm from war, he stood there – cutting the figure of perfect triumph. In the background, the tall bush stood with hints of bark lost in the thick, where faces could be made out, where branches twisted into arms bearing arms – the sky, streaked with banners of cloud.

Sunlight falls behind him, partially shadowing his stance. Trees in the distance, caressed by a light wind, their leaves alight with reds, mauve, pinks and fawn. And he stands tall, as though he'd invented this very moment: arm out on the windmill, the blades out of picture turning with the sound of metal cutting through air.

*

What great sense of wonder they gave us, climbing to the tops near the blades – a view of pleasure mixed with peril, the distance beneath our feet.

What gods we were when we found their replicas, how high we stood, what great games for towering colossi.

*

For hours we stationed ourselves on our bellies, blowing into windmills on the sand-coloured carpet, watching the metal sails rotate, hypnotised by the silver spin. We were caricatured clouds, full cheeks blowing westward, eastward, northward and south – the vanes performing simple magic from an exhale.

We competed to see who could turn the blades fastest – then shouted into the rotation to hear our voices cut, cut, cut… to fragments of loaded air – words sliced to coded messages, wisps of secrets.

And in our chants of nonsense I'd wish the world away, but the blades kept spinning, only to slow to a yielding pace that broke to a halt of silence.

*

Two days he lay silent in his grand cot, diminishing. The towering figure reduced to moments of awkward helplessness. His moist skin darkening like the earth we could not use by the vlei, where a stream dissipated into soft black soil, where bulrushes grew in the swale and dragonflies hovered through the putrid smell.

Near the windmill in the east, the bog was the first place we looked when one of the herd went astray. Its unforgiving centre held the beasts – never letting go, bulrushes and fen sedge drawing in their bodies, taking fatal hold.

And the nights now are for fear, great gasping fields of darkness without stars – whole hours of quicksand for the dying. Trees, souls locked to the earth, twisted with fear. And when the nights have passed, and the mornings come still – we ask the dawn, With what ills?

The bird keeping vigil.

III

As I turn from the window, to make my way to the door, all motion is slow motion as though the acacia field is moving.

In a car, as a child years ago, I stare out as speed propels a different field back: an orchard of oranges, trees in the thousands – fluorescent golf balls hurling through green branches, backward. In the field, late afternoon, a man labours with the full weight of a basket in his hands; he walks slowly, dissolving like a drawn-out shadow.

Those new days, their effervescence, as we explored the new country through every open road. Father's window rolled down, the car droning through time – slipstreamed and warm, its white bonnet cutting through air like a buoyant plank launching out of water.

A decade and a half on, I see the same old man shuffling through the fruit-field. His walk, redefined, his meaning – another meaning for being there. A man I shall know and never know my whole life as a bird crashes into the windscreen with the diminuendo of my mother's scream.

IV

It crept with the silence of light – then, with the speed of the wind, came rushing through the night with the sound of joints popping and bones snapping clean.

The fire-bell rang, its cold vibration – solid and thick. Its tone, shivering through flesh. Its sound – filled with urgency as waves of steel panic rung off with every pound of the iron bar.

Men dressed and scrambled into the night with wet sacks, stripping branches off any tree.

★

Like a distant nightmare it came in a dream. Fire, rising from the horizon, burning on its edge: a crown for that which will raise its fiery head and fill the dreamer with its light.

At the foot of the bed it appeared: translucent, pale and heavy – garnering no fear, summoning me to where we stood out beneath the evening sky: there, it held my hand as the moon and stars orbited its head.

With a long polished claw it pointed into the night – pointing far beyond reason, intellect and memory. What lay there was uncertain yet all too clear, a colourless mud; it offered to take me there, but on one condition: I shall go forever.

The lemur rolled the moon on its tongue, sucked softly, waiting for my reply. Its breath smelt of aniseed. It said nothing and still pointed *far beyond* with its arm bridging distance – offering it all; *as easy as that, as easy as crossing*
                              Distance
& what lies beyond distance, and transgresses all time.

Outside, tears streamed down my face – voices, and hands on my shoulders ushering me back: *But where to? Have I reached there?* or still walking back, bloody and wet – my father tucking me into the standby bed. The worn mattress suspending tomorrow indefinitely.

★

Dancers, curtains of flames – souls burning – flushing forward, pulling back – arms flinging, bodies melting in and bursting out. We stood before the dancers – faces bronze-hot, tractors heaving up – cutting fireguards behind us.

Chuff, smoke, the crackle and whistling of burning, deep in the heartland of the bush. Wet sacks and branches with seared leaves mopping up flames.

A strange dance in the wind – the fire pushing forward, men shuffling back from burning arms, then at their paces – forward, back – when the wind changed.

All night.

Dawn finally reclaimed the land as the field smouldered. The sweet smell of ash like powdered sugar beneath our feet. Tufts of grass crumbling with each step we took, our bodies torn by the effort – clothes matted to us with sweat.

All night – the dance.

★

No mirror apart from the effigy folding and unfolding in the basin. Ash in my palms, dusk-like and dusty. The bathroom, sombre – a distorted face undulating on the water as I stare clean into its depth.

Into the eye of water, within the chipped discoloured basin, his face peering back at me, his wholesome image staring from beneath the surface.

Carefully I place my hand to the reflection – lightly, so as not to cause a quiver or the slightest stir; so gently the water rises to my fingertips.

I feel his cheek, an unconscious brittle sound of stubble rustling through the air, remembering I kissed him there, upon those deep eddies of dimples whenever we parted for more than a day.

V

For two days his coffin lay in the living room, the room saturated with chants and wails, dirges and local hymns. Hosho spraying rhythm all night, the seeds and dry gourd accompanied by beating drums, the flare of a kudu-horn.

The coffin was lifted at dawn, the hearse waited in the driveway. The procession spooling out of the house like black thread, the needle the coffin. Around the household, through the yard, they carried him: through the orchard, the rose garden – past the swing, past the geyser with its metal door open, the cottage, and finally beneath the fir-tree.

The starling gone. The sky swollen with clouds.
Rain clouds.

Plastic anoraks were drums as raindrops thudded down on us. Each child separated by three feet of muddy earth as we dibbled a hole, placed the seed and covered.

Tynwald: a three-acre plot. The clouds had been threatening for days. A heavy, pregnant wind struggled over the field as we laboured days before. Its thick breath smelling of asphalt, wet bricks, dry tea leaves in a cup.

When the rain came, it slanted in shards shooting from the heavens; clear bolting comets pummelling our coloured anoraks. I looked to my brother doing the paces: one, two, three: hoe, plant, cover – and though the light was sombre, raindrops took on the colours of his anorak, forming a rainbow on the arch of his back.

Father, a child's mile ahead, by the boundary of the field, turned to us, angered at our slow pace. With water streaming down his face into his bearded chin, he shouted, droplets spurting from his lips, 'The last row! Then we'll all go into the house!'

All four sons; we hoed, planted and covered till the end of the field where the road, beyond the boundary, curved to an out-of-sight solitude. And even though he had done another row and told us to go indoors, he kept going with the fuel of the future.

Out in the field where maize would sprout and the sun suck the shoots into the sky – there he laboured in solitude: one, two, three – hoe, plant, cover.

*

Death led us along its path behind the hearse. The black chariot with curtained glass. Its tail-lights blinking – two scintillating stars: two stars in the constant mirage to my father's village.

Death lead us through the dust, past barbed-wire fences – to the pencil bushes of rural reservations, through groups of donkeys, cattle and herdsmen, through villages shaded beneath the deep blood-foliage of the mupfuti.

Two stars and I follow. A slow convoy trailing. A strange heavy taste in my mouth, the compass-needle of blood guiding me on, the family gravesite steering the wheels to where earth opens up with the wet breath of death.

★

On the mantelpiece, a verdite frame: a faded photograph depicts a young couple thronged by a motionless crowd – the crowd is singing, dancing beneath the eaves of a hut where dust has risen from bare feet and is now suspended in time for ever.

She holds flowers, the bride, dressed in white. The groom is all bravado – standing straight and sturdy like a tree-trunk severed just below its first branch. The best man, much smaller than him, looks to the ground as though he consults the groom's shadow, but in actuality is only whispering a joke.

And much the same as then – he looks down now, though no joke, into the grave – a throng of dancers singing and grieving as my father's coffin is lowered into the shadowed hole. My mother throws a lily to the descending casket, and both seemingly fall for ever.

VI

In the distance, the aquamarine glare from its eyes spilt into the night of a winter field. In the cold it stood, transfixed. Dart – begins the chase. Dust rumbling, billows churning in the wake of rusted metal – the car leaking oil, a trail of black slick seeping into earth, blood of the engine dense with the coming-killing knotted into the dust. The wheels – the murderous tread rolling on into the dart and jump – the night game of death. The chase. The hunt.

Song, blood-song – hypnotism by beating drum, the heart thudding – the fog in sheets of vaporous floe inches above the road, hiding, revealing the chase around the bend. Dark blades of grass flanking the roadside, gravel sparkling ahead with the fire in the chaser's eye. Jump, jump-jump – swerve, duck – wheel, skid, turn – dust spilling out over the curve. The crush of gravel beneath the wheels. Song, dead on will. Chase. Kill.

Madness condensed to a drop of rage. Full stop of words unsaid. Speed, blank as an empty page. All the world in the nip and dip of a rabbit's tail. Kill it. Kill the noise – kill the mad drum drumming mad to the beat and rhythm of blood. This mechanism blown to chaos, feeding the mind with thought – the needle slid so cleanly beneath the skin.

> Dear God,
> the shorn fields look so beautiful
> beneath the moonlight –
> a sea of blue earth,
> waves of loose sheaves
> from what the combine harvester
> shot out in chaff,
> shredded leaves and stalks
> floating silently through the wind.
>
> My father is there, he stands with his back to me,
> the debris falling like stars through the sky,
> his body a part of the hills – blue and distant.
>
> I call out to him from the boundary of the field
> where the road echoes. He doesn't hear me.
> I want him to stretch out his arms and have the chaff
>
> float all around him. He doesn't hear me.
> I want the moon and stars to rest on his palms.
> He doesn't hear me; instead, he walks to the pick-up,
>
> gets in and drives further down, over the slope
> into a quiet vlei – the red tail-lights
> disappearing out of sight.
>
> Dawn threatens the horizon with latent shapes
> and the moon begins to dissolve –
> its long dream-laced cloak wavering in the wind.

Stared too long. Stared. Hopelessly gasping for air. The chase still on. Headlights. Eyes taking time to adjust again. The drumming of palms on the steering-wheel. Song, blood-song,

the beating drum – the adrenaline – this endless road knowing
no route to heaven. The bobbing scut flashing in the headlights.
The windshield fogging up. Dart – swerve. The long chase, the
short corner rushing up.

As old as I, new beard dripping black from his chin,
dust in his eyes as he waves unperturbed,   waving and
mouthing, *Good-bye, good-bye, good-bye*
beside a tree as white and painless as aspirin.

VII

Death took all dignity from him, through its first and final
stages. His body curled like a foetus, his eyes rolled back:
desperately, infinitely, he gurgled for breath.

The heat drew on me as I wrestled to turn him over in
his bed, struggling to churn his weight.

★

One by one he would take us into his arms, cradle us for
a moment, rocking us: then from his god-like strength we were
flung like memories into the unsure as we were hurled up then
fell and splashed into the pool.

There was a safety and imagined danger in this game; he
stood at the edge of the pool like a machine manufacturing joy
as we ran into his arms like components into the assembly line
– to be flung into absolute completion, again.

★

Fields blurred past the car's windows, the car's speed
tested to the limit, time and distance tampering with the road.
Each bend we took – another stretch was invented, where time
stalled beneath the wheels.

The rubber road stretched on, gasps of life sucked out the
window to dissipate in the slipstream. What was a seven-minute
drive was now a lifetime's journey; the car turning off the

highway, tearing through the small town – burning the streets for the clinic.

★

Nurses on the lawn, knitting, reading magazines, having lunch, dozing in the shade beneath trees. Uniforms white as purity – their poise, a poise of pure ease.

One so easily missed it in the panic; others sat with them – staring emptily at the earth, counting grains in the sand, propped up in the shade, fading on trunks of trees.

The car pulled in, doors flying open before the actual stop – a throw of panic in upheld arms – only body-language through loss of words. But no one came. Uniforms white as purity – their poise, a poise of pure ease.

No weight could question my strength – my hands locked over my father's chest, his back on my stomach, his loose head, as we carried him into the clinic.

VIII

The air filled with sparkling flight, a whole field gently rising with wings. Rain had fallen, the horizon clear – the sun sinking, its red heavy light loaded with dreams. November and the first sense of real rain – flying ants taking to the air in fields where a team of tractors once worked from dawn till evening; now – hazel tufts of scattered grass and orange anthills make the landscape.

In the evening light, I stop the pick-up and get out to run through the field of wings – my arms out beneath the sky streaked with an aftertaste of blood – wet soil picking up and flicking from my boots. Soon, there will be a full moon, and at first it will be blood red as the sun is now, and blunt like the crown of a stillborn.

As I run, three feathered shadows stand with shadows on open ground – the buzzards' heads nodding, twisting in the flight of ants. Their feast, a strange, portentous dance. And dusk,

dusk claims the shapes, draining them into other shapes fused with black – this field, the same field years back where all seven of us walked, having no choice but to trust the dark. The endless depth of that night – a great vault where cloud cover performed illusions through the sky: pulling the whole world in, making the whole world disappear. And in that darkness was our fear, right down to the scent of mud, our feet drudging through the bog, calls of night-birds, wild dogs and jackals piercing our hearts then withdrawing like pins out of velvet cushions.

We walked, whichever way we thought the homestead was; my father almost primal. The Land Rover stuck in the distance – a presence, a dead emotion curled up in the corner of a dream.

For days it had rained, mud caked our boots and dragged us down. The weight, with each step we took, gathered – drawing on the body with a root of gravity you had to break again and again. I feared stopping and being planted in the mud – white blind roots spreading out from my toes – knees locked, and legs stiffening.

The buzzards lifted to a dead tree. Monstrous wingspans flapping over new stars and planets. What had I done? All around me still the hypnotic fluttering of ants. And in the last bits of bruised sky – silhouettes of swifts and bats – I raise my hands and fall protecting my head from a large crude shape.

The sound of the wet grass slashes through my ears as I roll through the sharpness – the field turning and trembling, I fear his gasping will stop, the loud labour of his breath cease and bring in the ultimate silence while all

IX

the ward watches as though it were a picture show starring father and son. Sweat from my face dripping into his, fingers caught to the bone between his teeth.

Breathe.

A cough in the ward here and there, clearings of throats, a word or two exchanged by neighbours in adjoining beds, spectators rolling over on sheets tanned by sweat.

He drowned in his own fluid. Sweat from my face raining into his.

All eyes on us.

★

★

The first film my father and I watched together was *Steptoe and Son*, in an old red-carpeted theatre. The smell of popcorn and pipe tobacco; the great casual upholstered seats that nearly lost me in their depth – the way they flipped up and had my naked knees on my chin; how I stuck my head up struggling to see the screen – and for the first time heard an audience burst out in the dark, laughing.

Credence

We found ourselves staring at the truck, the trucker staring back,
the gearbox, driveshaft or something else seriously fucked, the truck's
hull loaded down with ore. No sign of traffic for miles – the road
offering nothing but the glare off jagged rocks, pyramids of black
      chrome gleaming in surrounding fields.

Eye to eye in the passing stare – stranger to stranger – a thought
to stop corrects itself with a deep suspicion time has brought
to bear from the common hand of man. Men like us who've never
seen real war know nothing of the swollen, bursting bodies caught
      in an unforgiving stronghold, the dead

waking gibbering veterans sweat-laced and cold. Even the hardened
scream, walking dream-fields, cradling rifles and axes – burdened
by the lie that time heals all; three generations die shackled by
the ethics of war. The trucker waves. But we have burned
      this meaning, silenced any credence of its code.

Flight

He kept running. Miles of emptiness, heat
and jagged stones wouldn't stop him. His feet
bled. His swollen tongue filled his mouth. Forget
them. How could he. How could he forget
their screams, the canned echoes off concrete

walls. As the blind hand of the sun beat
down on him, he knew they were dead. The heat
quickened his heart with thirst and fear – yet
he kept running.

For days he'd had nothing proper to eat.
He thought of Tendai, how they nearly beat
her to death when they found him; he should have let
her know. He thought of their last night when the threat
of death vanished as they fucked in the heat.
He kept running.

Water

1

Blue crane stalk harrowed fields.
     The sky bannered with a platinum heat.
Fondling a palm-full of putty, the explosives expert jokes:
    This shit could raze Parliament.

          Fire in the hole.
     Fire in the hole.
       Fire in the hole.

     Firing now.

Like brown flour sifted in a sieve,
     earth shifts up before the muscled boom.
The crew, high on adrenaline, pop up from the bunker,
pumping fists with jokes of this being a purely masculine thing:
     making the earth move,
       like making women scream.

2

    Barsaat would like anything – anything green.
    Asks if I'd consider horticulture for his grocery
    in Belvedere; wooden crates, assorted beans
    flushed open on metal shelves. *Mung?* The lean
    man enquires, nodding his head with the query.

    Barsaat, a farmer years back in Selous, regrets
    nothing, loves the land still: wheat germ husks
    dry as electricity, diesel oil and manure, egrets
    on troughs, kestrels hovering over red sunsets,
    green flowering fields; recalling all this he asks,

    Just how much water do you have?

3

In a natural bull-horned arrangement, dunned eucalyptus trunks
        sleep beside black granite rocks, a party of relatives
and friends sit on the bays set decades and centuries back.

A patient priest, gilded robes, guides the couple through vows
        beside short pomegranate trees pregnant with fruit.
A weak sulking rain draws a thin curtain across the lake,

silver gossamer over Norton town. Farmers and farming wives
        all certain the shower heads off west to Darwendale.
And so it does, as casual as the groom kisses the bride.

Guests eat. Whiskey eases painful speeches under a tent
        out of someone's barn. Wild geese on grass honk loud
in the sweet mosquito heat we were born in.

A bruised purple sheen stains the lake's surface, a worked misery
        echoing into the museum of age. A small plane
flies hard to beat darkness. A shower of rose petals blisters the lake.

4

The beasts charged in.
Two hundred head.
        All hoof and bone
churning charred dust
in the hazelnut paddock.

The first half of the run,
driving beasts through fields
        taller than men,
herders whistling over
laboured lows.

Two miles of stolen wire.
Cattle troughs bone dry,
a pair of tyre-

sandals over bales
of copper coiled dead

in the grass – an insult
to every effort, every death
    of every calf,
every bull and cow.
The crude wire-cutters

simply abandoned.
Day after day, the bellowing,
    death's bond
on sunset and sunrise,
wax hides tight on bone.

Running ahead to check
the dam's banks, the cattle
    fall back –
herdsmen's shouts
softened by distance.

There, on the banks, a cool
silence – peppery smells,
    a flock of teal
busying the water, snipe
scurrying on luminous

silver moss, islands thick
with reeds running the illusion
    of drifting back;
dead treetops playing along
with grey startled arms.

A darter, dark and slick,
spreads its wings to dry –
    oiled and Christ-like,
a family on the opposite
bank walks as though

a world apart from here
could not exist. Then, hoof fall:
     drumming thunder:
ash and dust
bitter on the tongue.

The Apostle

Returning from the pool, the great white bull
turns to the cross-hairs, the mountain path
curving with the gathered rush of a waterfall

tumbling over dolerite in the distance. Heath
shivers, blue steam rising with the pale sun,
the thin morning air white off the bull's breath.

With the beast locked in the sight's focal plane,
time fell still, the valley below glowing bright
as river water carved rock silver with motion.

The apostle stood. All sculpted muscle. White
hide, blanched chevron bridging the brow,
spirited eyes fired with a burning Fahrenheit.

No fracture in distance could part them now.
Chance and time cancelling the blood's fast
throb, eye to eye, the gentle stain of shadows

thickening. Bushshrikes whistled, the first
sweet notes clear with a lust for life, and there –
in the music of mountain light and bush mist,

perfumes of wild loquat burst ripe in the air.
The bull genuflected and fell. The waterfall's
rush gathering the sun deep in the albino's ear.

The Reduction

Across the service road, block-faced tractors carve fields
into narrow ridged lanes. Dust trails rise from the furrows,
curling above paddocks licked gold with windswept grass.
The vet takes off his shirt, browns his arms to the elbows;
standing back – he studies the cow's prolapsed womb,
palms level with his chest in some sort of medical prayer.

After a moment's thought, the sun beating hard on his back,
he leans in to cradle the womb with a mastered stoicism.
Gently he purges the muscle of grass and earth, rust-red water
flowing down her hocks, her head locked in the steel spasm
of the crush, eyes lost in the rolling shine of paddocks.
Pale signatures of dust scrawl the sky, the whispered strokes

vanishing into a blue canvas. In the pen, her day-old calf
springs about on giddy legs, the black calf shiny as split coal.
A whirlwind rises, stirring up dust and flamboyant petals.
Again, the gentle bath; but first a warm slap, a fresh bowl
and murmurs of song; his battered box open, needles, blades
and bottles spinning hypnotic webs of light over his elbow.

He shaves the base of the cow's tail. Slides the needle in.
He lifts the bright muscle, but pain dismantles her stance,
so he waits – blowflies glittering in the heat like emeralds,
her braced dance, swaying, gradually returning her balance.
Then, with an assured commitment, he guides the uterus in.
Everything beneath the sun gives stage to loud sequential farting,

a sherry rush of liquid courses down the vet's arm, into his
armpit, down his flank, to his work-trousers – the pale fluid
forming faint maps. Purposeful and red, a steady rain of petals
falls. The polished hum of bees bright beside the grading shed.
And as delicate as light salted by the sun, wafts of medicine
and dust ride the air with a perfume the whole scene needs.

Open Country

Shortwave crackles through the open countryside,
      cattle bells ringing-in the evening news.
Paraffin throws its dirty light as memories fall
         into walls scarred with shared history.

Sweet churned smells from thick illicit brews
quietly drown the widower's fatigue. The rural clock
      works fast over termite-infested furniture.
Limbs sprawled on the naked floor. The wood stove

      resting, silently bricked with white cinder.
The wind ringing cold with a dry bitter interlude.

Mercantile Rain

Before all sorts of retro disco struts or *robot-moves* begin,
before seventies cover songs and empty crates of champagne,
the cake comes in sparkling bright with candles from an age
blessed with every success garnered from this new life.
The colonel stands, lifting his glass. The tent's raised stage
rocked by thunder – earth and sky fast flicked with a knife-
     white light drawing out the long squeal of the microphone…

True perfumes smell like insect repellent in this weather.
An early dinner, long birthday speeches before the thunder
landed its haunting echo, the colonel's loss of words, flute
up in the air like a crystal arum on fire against the pregnant
horizon. Once young and bell-cheeked, proud and resolute,
the colonel said to his wife, *We must leave here after the rains,*
     because the war is coming. And so the war came –

loud with every death, dark with every monstrous fear.
No one survived, except him. Wife and son ambushed near
the border, brother silent since crossing to Mozambique,
mother buried in a bricked-up well; and when the Runde
swells, villagers can still taste the blood, the river's sick
black cream. And he remembers his wife nodding, thunder
     folding over the hut, fields bright with burning cane.

So they dance, the sweet lawn dry beneath the canvas tent,
music and French wine, the whispering rain the bold servant
of old memories. And the cover songs know no family but
the large room he sleeps alone in, troubled by grieving, dead
drunk, lost in the heated valley that floods his heart – the hot
blood of men oiling his grip, the war still ruling his bed,
     wet with squeals carved beneath his brother's cheekbones…

Now the Boy's Not Coming Along

It's the afternoon tea that eventually had to come someday, somehow.
Now that he thinks of it – nothing's strange about how everything
fell into place like a plan: car battery flat at his aunt's bungalow –
her husband out at the club attempting to shoot an eagle in the rain.
Of all days to visit, he drives in at the same time his grandfather's
second wife easily shifts the proud old man from the car to his chair,
freckled hands trembling, shielding his face from the heavens' spit.

The plan: in-and-out in less than ten minutes, give them no time
to conspire, but he's too late, time allies with the day's conspiracy
as a frayed electrical wire shorts – bleeding the car battery dry.
After packing in his mother's weekend bags, wary of the time,
her face lights up with a wry smile when the key turns to a sifted
cough forcing every light on the dash to resign. Goodbye waves
turn to urgent arms hauling them in even before the bonnet's lifted.

The call: wait till the rain stops. Here hierarchy runs threefold,
respect by default, nothing's left unresolved in these proud homes.
Polished teaspoons slip through amber tea. Conversations unfold
after tradition honours ceremony. Homemade gingerbread and scones
lie sweet on Aynsley China. A sober command turns women out
to the kitchen where steam-curled recipes for *Divas with Gout*
ply the walls below daily prayers. With the women gone, the room

clear, the old man turns to him. Grips his hand. Speaks in his ear.
Enthusiasm between them is all but gone. His grandfather taught
him chess when he was young, recited Donne, Hopkins, Herbert…
But now the boy's not coming along, he fears all will disappear
without a wife or God. But God does not work as he should in our
time, religious talk will not save the bloodline. With a heavy heart
the young man listens. Each desperate whisper falling dry and sour.

Hat-trick

Barefoot, the boy runs down the road,
arms out like a plane, swerving side to side
      with a group of boys chasing him.
            It's all screams and laughter, the sun
piercing jacarandas, shallow pools of bullion-
      light bubbling flat in the shade.

Old studio flats stand gutted, the reflection
of paned glass replaced by dull plastic sheets.
      From the bar across the road, men
            accompany women into Sadler's Court,
re-emerging alone, holding brown quarts
      of beer with a light-footed absence.

A milky stream flows along the roadside.
Scum-curdled odours rise thick and rich and ride
      the dirty air with a stubborn charge,
            pot-holed sidewalks littered with debt
beside Mohawks of grass growing lush yet
      sickly with a tainted ashen sheen.

On the corner of the street: up-ended bins,
a murder of crows beside young men washing
      cars for close to nothing. So the boy runs in,
            left arm palming the air, right arm straight –
releasing the ball to split the beer crate
      they had used as stumps.

Facsimile of a Quiet Country

Fungal spore and rusty pollen
    catch your breath along with the view.
Every footstep weighed after every stride taken, wood-
    tiled floor giving in, soft as dung. Drizzle
falls through fire-chewed timber, each charred angle
        locked in silent degrees shadowed by the temperature

of mist slowly filling the ruin.
    The house stands empty. Gutted black.
This room, a room where a couple once woke refreshed by love,
    or trapped in discomforts marriage fails
to cure. A charred wooden doll, driven with nails,
        lies exposed in the corner, its torn limbs scattered black

beside nuggets of human shit.
    You can hear it all, how it happened,
if you listen. The missing wall, loud with noise, replaced by the view
    of the sun setting over hills rolling quietly
through midland country, bright fawn foliage gently
        whispering through the leaves, the leaves whispering back.

The doors are gone. Door and frame.
    Charcoaled graffiti bitches over history.
One comment stands alone, scored in thick capitals –
    FUCK YOU AND ALL YOUR LIES!
Soiled palm prints smudged flat around the phrase,
        thin finger-trails streaking down to the missing skirting.

The river below meanders beneath the mist.
    The sun a red miserable glow faint with a silence
this season gives, a spiritual silence wet with flying ants staining
    broken glass, the delicate song of rain
singing through broken trusses, up to where pain
        opens its wings to soar through skies quietened by height.

Zvita

Study the bone. The waxed coat stiff with flies.
    Dark corroded holes, missing eyes
sucking light into a cave of teeth, gypsum-white
on black, rigid tongue lost above a lung of steel.
Down the jaw, yellow flume – the slow, slick gel
    of albumen flowing over death's chalice,
down the belly's protruding cavity. A red termite
mound hitches the spine cruelly. The back's awkward
arch parting rigid legs, pushing the pelvis forward
    to give birth to death's black oozing grease.
Labour is drawn; silent as hoof and horn. Stones
bake flat on the valley's hearth. Sinew on bone
lies wet in a slick private darkness, rich suet
    soups warm around muscle till a blanket
of white work carves the skeleton out. Sun and rain
blend perfumes we never trust. The ancient oils
of life, rich with spent secretions, returned to soil –
anointing a seed unfurled through the pelvic crown.